THE FLYING DUTCHMAN

THE DOOMED GHOST SHIP

BY MEGAN COOLEY PETERSON

CAPSTONE PRESS
a capstone imprint

Snap Books are published by Capstone Press, an imprint of Capstone.
1710 Roe Crest Drive
North Mankato, Minnesota 56003
www.capstonepub.com

Library of Congress Cataloging-in-Publication Data is available on the Library of Congress website.

ISBN: 978-1-5435-7338-1 (hardcover)
ISBN: 978-1-4966-6611-6 (paperback)
ISBN: 978-1-5435-7347-3 (eBook PDF)

Summary: The ghost ship the Flying Dutchman has been spotted around the world for centuries. According to legend, this spooky ship is doomed to roam the seas forever, unable to make port. The ship is thought to be a bad omen for anyone who encounters it. Dating back to the 1600s, alleged sightings of the legendary ghost ship continue to this day.

Image Credits

Alamy: Antiqua Print Gallery, 18, Cayman, 25, incamerastock, 7, Kentish Dweller, 23, KGPA Ltd, 20-21, Panther Media GmbH, 14; Getty Images: Arkivi, 13; iStockphoto: duncan1890, 12; Newscom: Tomo Ikic/ZUMA Press, 19; Shutterstock: Alfredo Schaufelberger, 16, avtk, Design Element, breakermaximus, 17, Chantal de Bruijne, Design Element, Dino Osmic, 5, 15, Elenarts, 22, Esteban De Armas, 27, Giraphics, Design Element, GoMixer, Design Element, Joseph M. Arseneau, 24, Kostyantyn Ivanyshen, 29, MagicDogWorkshop, Design Element, muratart, 9, NikhomTreeVector, Design Element, Oliver Denker, 10, Paul Yates, 28, PLRANG ART, Cover, Room 76, 4, trekandshoot, 11, wanderlust86, 8

Editorial Credits

Editor: Eliza Leahy; Designers: Lori Bye and Brann Garvey; Media Researcher: Tracy Cummins; Production Specialist: Kathy McColley

Direct Quotations

page 19: Steiger, Brad. *Real Ghosts, Restless Spirits, and Haunted Places.* Canton, MI: Visible Ink Press, 2003, 484.

All internet sites appearing in back matter were available and accurate when this book was sent to press.

Printed and bound in the USA.   PA99

TABLE OF CONTENTS

A GHOSTLY SHIP

It's sunset, and you're hanging out with your family at the beach. A cool breeze blows off the ocean waves. Someone lights a fire and roasts marshmallows. As you look across the water, a ship appears on the horizon. Its sails look tattered and torn. As it moves closer to shore, the ship fades. Before you can point it out to your family, the ship vanishes. Did you just witness the *Flying Dutchman* ghost ship?

Ghost ships have been reported around the world for hundreds of years. The *Flying Dutchman* is one of the most famous ghost ships. According to legend, this ghost ship and the **spirits** on board are doomed. They are forced to roam the seas forever. The sight of the *Dutchman* is said to bring bad luck. It is also said that a *Dutchman* sighting can sink a ship. **Skeptics** believe these sightings are likely fog or real ships mistaken for the *Dutchman*. Read on to decide if the *Flying Dutchman* is more than just a ghost story.

4

FACT

The movie *Pirates of the Caribbean: Dead Man's Chest* features the *Flying Dutchman*.

CHAPTER ONE

THE LEGEND OF THE *FLYING DUTCHMAN*

The story of the *Flying Dutchman* has been told for hundreds of years. No one knows for sure if it was a real ship. There are many different versions of the story. One of the most common tales begins in 1641. A Dutch captain named Hendrick van der Decken sailed his ship between the Netherlands in Europe and islands in Southeast Asia called the East Indies. The ship belonged to the Dutch East India Company. It brought back spices and silks to the Netherlands.

Captain van der Decken and his crew had left the East Indies without trouble. But their luck changed as they continued their journey. On their way back to the Netherlands, the captain decided to sail around the Cape of Good Hope in South Africa. It was the quickest route home—but also the most dangerous. That area of sea was known to be difficult to cross. Still, van der Decken pressed on.

The Dutch East India Company was located in Amsterdam.

FACT

One of the first written stories about the *Flying Dutchman* was published in 1821. It appeared in *Blackwood's Edinburgh Magazine*.

As the *Dutchman* sailed around the Cape of Good Hope,
a violent storm blew in. Rain and wind blasted the ship.
Captain and crew battled the weather for weeks with no
forward progress. The crew begged the captain to turn back.
But van der Decken refused to listen.

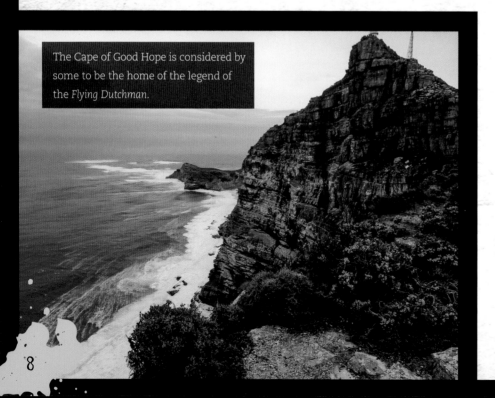

The Cape of Good Hope is considered by
some to be the home of the legend of
the *Flying Dutchman*.

In the midst of the storm, the crew supposedly saw God appear as an image in the sky. His image signaled that the ship should turn back. The sailors fell to their knees. But van der Decken fired his pistol toward the **apparition**. He vowed to make his way through the storm, no matter the cost. Legend has it that van der Decken and his crew were forced to sail forever on their **phantom** ship, never reaching shore.

SKEPTIC'S NOTE

Stories of the *Flying Dutchman* are **inconsistent**. The ship's captain has different names depending on the story. He is sometimes called Cornelius instead of Hendrick, and sometimes his last name is spelled "Vanderdecken." If the story were true, the details wouldn't change.

OTHER VERSIONS

Other versions of the *Flying Dutchman* change some key details. In one, van der Decken and only one crewman were doomed to the sea. Van der Decken himself was turned into a monster.

PLAYING DICE WITH THE DEVIL

A tale similar to the *Flying Dutchman* comes from Germany. According to the legend, Captain Falkenberg had committed murder. The devil appeared on his ship and challenged Falkenberg to a game of dice. Falkenberg lost, and the devil claimed his soul. The captain was forced to sail the North Sea forever.

In another tale, the *Dutchman* chases other ships. Once the *Dutchman* catches a ship, van der Decken leans over the rail. His ghostly hand holds out a letter. He begs the living sailors to mail it for him. But according to legend, touching the letter brings bad luck. No sailor will mail it.

FACT

According to a 2012 poll, 45 percent of Americans believe in ghosts.

CHAPTER TWO

ENCOUNTERING THE *FLYING* DUTCHMAN

The *Flying Dutchman* may have sunk in the 1600s. But people have **allegedly** spotted the ghostly ship ever since. Even British royalty have encountered the ghost ship. Could the legend be true? Or are witnesses confusing clouds, fog, or other ships with the *Dutchman*?

A ROYAL ENCOUNTER

In 1881, Prince George of Wales was sailing on the HMS *Inconstant* near Australia. The ship was part of the Royal Navy. Around 4:00 a.m. on July 11, a strange red light appeared on the sea. The light was about 200 yards from the *Inconstant*. In the light's center were the **masts** and sails of a ship.

As the ship came alongside the *Inconstant*'s **port** side, it suddenly faded away. Two nearby ships, the *Tourmaline* and the *Cleopatra*, messaged the *Inconstant*. Crew on those ships had also seen the red light. Many sailors believed they had just seen the *Dutchman*.

Later that morning, things took a deadly turn. A sailor who had been climbing the *Inconstant*'s **rigging** fell to his death. This same sailor first reported seeing the *Dutchman*. Had the cursed ship claimed another victim? Or was it only a **coincidence**?

SKEPTIC'S NOTE

Scientists say that certain ocean temperatures can bend light waves around the earth's curve. These bending light waves can make objects *beyond* the horizon visible. Sailors may have seen a real ship just beyond the horizon, not a ghost ship.

The HMS *Inconstant* was built in 1869. From 1869–1871, the ship was part of the Channel Squadron that defended the English Channel.

THE *ORKNEY BELLE*

The *Orkney Belle*, a Scottish whaling ship, was sailing near Iceland in January 1911. Soon, another ship came into view. The name *Flying Dutchman* was painted on its **stern**. Winds swelled the ship's sails. But the crew aboard the *Orkney Belle* said there was no wind that day. Suddenly, a bell rang three times from deep within the strange ship. Then the *Flying Dutchman* disappeared into the mist.

SWIMMERS BEWARE

In 1939, swimmers on South Africa's coast got more than just surf and sun. Dozens of swimmers reported seeing the *Flying Dutchman*. Witnesses all described an old-fashioned ship with masts and sails. As the crowd watched, the ship disappeared into thin air. Had they seen the *Flying Dutchman*? Or was there another explanation?

SKEPTIC'S NOTE

Fog could be mistaken for a ghostly ship.

THE HMS *JUBILEE*

On August 3, 1942, the British ship HMS *Jubilee* was sailing near Cape Town, South Africa. Around 9:00 p.m., naval officers saw a strange ship sailing on the horizon. Its sails were raised, and the ship was being pushed by wind. But like on the *Orkney Belle*, the officers said there was no wind that night. When they tried to contact the ship, it gave no reply. The *Jubilee* even had to change course to avoid a crash. Then the ship vanished. Had the sailors narrowly avoided the *Flying Dutchman*?

CAUGHT ON FILM?

Modern reports of the *Flying Dutchman* are rare. One of the most recent sightings occurred in 2012. A man began filming the sunset off the coast of Wales. As he watched the sunset, something else appeared. A glowing shape floated in the sky. The man zoomed in, trying to get a better look. He believed he may have captured the *Flying Dutchman* on film.

SKEPTIC'S NOTE

Flying Dutchman sightings always place the ship in the water. No previous witnesses have said the ship was flying in the sky.

CHAPTER THREE

GHOST SHIPS AROUND THE WORLD

The *Flying Dutchman* isn't the only ship to have met a violent end, then come back to haunt the seas. On March 24, 1878, the HMS *Eurydice* was sailing near the Isle of Wight in England. The seas were calm. Suddenly, the three-masted naval ship was caught in a surprise storm. Snow, ice, and strong winds lashed the ship. The captain had no time to prepare, and the ship sank. All but two of the 360 men on board died.

But that would not be the last time the *Eurydice* set sail.

The HMS *Eurydice* was returning from a three-month voyage when it sank.

On rainy nights, the HMS *Eurydice* is said to reappear. Many sailors have reported seeing this ghostly ship. In 1998, Prince Edward of Wales was filming a TV show on the Isle of Wight. Prince Edward and the crew were discussing the *Eurydice*. Suddenly, a three-masted ship appeared on the horizon. The crew thought it looked similar to the *Eurydice* and began filming it. But then the ship disappeared.

Had the television crew seen a ghost ship? Prince Edward was convinced they had. "There are too many stories, coincidences, occurrences, and strange happenings," he said of the experience. "There is definitely something out there. . . . I cannot believe it is just people's imagination."

Prince Edward founded his own television production company, Ardent Productions, in 1993.

FACT

Another ship, the *Emma*, was about a mile behind the *Eurydice* when it sank. The *Emma* never encountered the storm.

THE *QUEEN MARY*

The *Queen Mary* carried guests around the world from 1936 to 1967. But this ocean liner has a dark past. During World War II, it carried American soldiers to and from Europe. The ship was painted gray and nicknamed the "Gray Ghost." The ship may have been chased by the Nazis. But the *Queen Mary*'s speed easily evaded Nazi U-boats.

In 1942, the *Queen Mary*'s speed and stealth caused a tragedy. The ship accidentally hit its escort ship, the HMS *Curacoa*. The *Curacoa* was sliced in two and sank near the coast of Ireland. Most of its crew drowned.

In 1967, the *Queen Mary* sailed to Long Beach, California. It was docked and turned into a permanent hotel. Strange things soon began happening on the *Queen Mary*. Guests reported seeing ghosts, objects moving on their own, and eerie lights floating up and down the hallways. The sound of metal crunching and people screaming has been heard near the ship's **bow**. Could it be the ghosts of those who died on the *Curacoa*?

FACT

At least 41 passengers and 16 crewmembers died on the *Queen Mary* while it was an ocean liner. They died from diseases and accidents. One crewman was allegedly crushed to death in a heavy metal door.

The *Queen Mary* made more than a thousand trips across the Atlantic Ocean before it was converted into a hotel.

THE *CALEUCHE* GHOST SHIP

Each night, a ghost ship allegedly sails off the coast of Chile's Chiloé Island. Witnesses say the *Caleuche* is a glowing white color. Its sails are as red as blood. This ship can speed across the water and even dive below the surface. As the ship passes by, the laughter of its dead crew can be heard. Some say witches live on the *Caleuche*. They can leave the ship by riding a magical seahorse. Many people believe the *Caleuche* guards the sea.

At its largest, the Goodwin Sands covers an area of about ten miles in length and three miles in width.

THE *LADY LOVIBOND*

In 1748, the captain of the *Lady Lovibond* took his new bride on a cruise. The captain's first mate was allegedly in love with the captain's wife. In a fit of jealousy, the first mate steered the *Lady Lovibond* onto the Goodwin Sands. This area of the English Channel has shifting sands. At low tide, they're just below the water's surface. Many ships have sunk there, and the *Lady Lovibond* met the same fate. Everyone on board died.

The *Lady Lovibond* is said to return every 50 years. The ghost ship reportedly runs **aground** on the Sands. Then the *Lovibond* vanishes before passing ships can send help.

FACT

More than 1,000 ships have sunk on the Goodwin Sands.

THE FIRE SHIP OF CHALEUR BAY

In Chaleur Bay, Canada, a terrifying ghost ship is said to haunt the waters. Witnesses have reported seeing a flaming ship on the water near Bathurst, New Brunswick. Even a former mayor claims to have seen the phantom ship.

A few legends attempt to explain the ghostly ship. According to one story, the ship's crew kidnapped a young bride. Seeking revenge, the locals set their ship on fire. The crew was doomed to sail forever. In another tale, two brothers kidnapped local women to sell as slaves and set off to sea. When they returned the following year, the locals were waiting for them. They drowned one of the brothers. The other brother set fire to the ship. He vowed to haunt Chaleur Bay for a thousand years.

SKEPTIC'S NOTE

Scientists say glowing gases can be mistaken for the Fire Ship of Chaleur Bay.

THE *MARY CELESTE*

The *Mary Celeste* was found abandoned on
December 5, 1872, near Santa Maria Island. This
island is west of Portugal. The ship had been sailing
from New York to Italy. Its sails were up, but there
was no one on board. The lifeboat was also gone.
But the ship still had plenty of food. The crew of the
Mary Celeste was never found.

A monument to the Mary Celeste can be
found on Spencer's Island in Nova Scotia.

CHAPTER FOUR

WAS THE FLYING DUTCHMAN A REAL SHIP?

The legend of the *Flying Dutchman* has captivated people for hundreds of years. It's been featured in books and movies. But was the *Dutchman* ever a real ship? Or is the tale told to warn people about the dangers of the sea?

Some historians suggest the *Dutchman* legend may have been based on a real person. In the 1600s, a man named Bernard Fokke sailed for the Dutch East India Company. Fokke was known for his speed at sea. At that time, some believed the devil helped him achieve such speed. According to the rumors, after Fokke's death he had to give his soul to the devil. Fokke was then forced to sail the seas for all time.

LEGENDS OF THE SEA

Sailors have long believed in many mythical creatures thought to lurk in the oceans. Mermaids were half fish, half human. Chasing a mermaid, sailors thought, could sink a ship. The half-bird, half-woman **siren** had a beautiful singing voice. Sailors who listened would forget to eat and die of starvation, or they might drown or wreck their ships. The famous **kraken** was a giant sea monster who was believed to drag ships to their watery graves.

SAILING DANGEROUS SEAS

Life at sea can be dangerous. The weather can change quickly, and ships can sink. In the past, many sailors had **superstitions** they believed could help them avoid disaster. Long ago, they cut holes in the sails of their ships. They thought evil spirits haunted the seas and didn't want them to get caught in the sails. Sailors never whistled on board a ship for fear of angering a sea god. Bananas were not allowed on board. They were considered unlucky and could cause a ship to get lost at sea.

The *Flying Dutchman* is just one of many myths and legends about traveling the sea. Davy Jones's locker is one of the most famous sea legends. According to the tale, Davy Jones lives at the bottom of the ocean. He keeps treasures and even dead sailors in his locker. Many sailors thought they would go to Davy Jones's locker if they died at sea.

These legends likely helped sailors feel more in control while at sea. They taught sailors what *not* to do. The *Flying Dutchman* may be only a spooky story. Or it may have been a real ship, doomed to sail for all time. Either way, it can be fun to imagine what could have happened.

GLOSSARY

aground (UH-ground)—stuck on land or on the bottom of a body of water

allegedly (uh-LEJ-id-ly)—having been said to be true without offering proof

apparition (ap-uh-RISH-uhn)—the visible appearance of a ghost

bow (BAU)—the very front of a ship

coincidence (koh-IN-si-duhns)—something that happens accidentally at the same time as something else

inconsistent (in-kuhn-SIS-tuhnt)—not continuing to happen or develop in the same way

kraken (KRAH-kuhn)—a legendary sea monster said to exist off the coast of Norway

mast (MAST)—a tall pole on a ship's deck that holds the sails

phantom (FAN-tuhm)—something that appears to be real but is not

port (PORT)—the left side of a ship looking forward

rigging (RIG-ing)—the system of ropes, chains, or wires that support and control the sails on a ship

siren (SYE-ruhn)—half-bird, half-woman creature that lures sailors to them by singing

skeptic (SKEP-tik)—someone who doubts or questions beliefs

spirit (SPIHR-it)—the invisible part of a person that contains thoughts and feelings; some people believe the spirit leaves the body after death

stern (STERN)—the back half of a ship

superstition (soo-pur-STI-shuhn)—a belief that an action can affect the outcome of a future event

READ MORE

Felix, Rebecca. *Ghosts: The Truth Behind History's Spookiest Spirits.* North Mankato, MN: Capstone Press, 2016.

Ramsey, Grace. *Haunted Ships, Planes, and Cars.* Vero Beach, FL: Rourke Educational Media, 2016.

Winters, Jaime. *Haunted at Sea.* New York: Crabtree Publishing Company, 2018.

INTERNET SITES

The Legend of the Flying Dutchman
https://www.ancient-origins.net/myths-legends/legend-flying-dutchman-ghostly-apparition-ship-captain-hendrick-007285

The Queen Mary
https://www.queenmary.com/history/timeline/the-creative-years/

Five Famous Ghost Ships
https://www.boatingmag.com/five-famous-ghost-ships

INDEX